Life Cycle of a

Salmon

Angela Royston

Heinemann Library
Chicago, Illinois

Customer Service 888-454-2279

Designed by Celia Floyd
Illustrated by Alan Fraser
Printed in China by South China Printing Co. Ltd.

04 03 02 01
10 9 8 7 6 5 4 3 2

Library of Congress Cataloging-in-Publication Data
Royston, Angela.
    Life cycle of a salmon / Angela Royston.
        p. cm.
    Includes bibliographical references (p.) and index.
    Summary: Introduces the life cycle of a sockeye salmon, as they swim from the river in which they were hatched to the sea and back again.
    ISBN 1-57572-212-7 (lib. bdg.)
    1. Salmon—Life cycles—Juvenile literature. [1. Salmon.] I. Title
QL638.S2R69 2000
597.5'6—dc21   99-046104

Acknowledgments
The Publisher would like to thank the following for permission to reproduce photographs:

Ardea London/Francois Gohier, p.19; Ardea London/Jean-Paul Ferrero, p. 4; Natalie B. Fobes, pp. 10, 12; Bruce Coleman Collection/Fred Bruemmer, p. 11; Bruce Coleman Collection/Jeff Foott, pp. 5, 24, 25; Bruce Coleman Collection/Johnny Johnson, p. 21; Pacific Stock, p. 26; Corbis, pp. 17, 18, 27; FLPA/D. Maslowski, p. 14, FLPA/Gerard Lacz, p. 15; Heather Angel, p. 20; Oxford Scientific Films/Jeff Foott, pp. 6, 7, 8, 23; Oxford Scientific Films/Martyn Chillmaid, p. 16; Planet Earth Pictures/Allan Parker, p. 13; Wildlife Matters, pp. 9, 22.

Cover photograph: Corbis

Some words are shown in bold, **like this.** You can find out what they mean by looking in the glossary.

Contents

What Is a Salmon?

A salmon is a fish. Some fish, such as these trout, live only in **freshwater** rivers or lakes. Other kinds of fish live only in the **salt water** of the sea.

Alevin

Fry

Smolt

Salmon are **unique.** They live part
of their lives in fresh water and part
in the salty sea. This book is about
the life of a **sockeye** salmon.

Fully grown

Going home

Spawning

Alevin

In autumn, a female fish laid this nest of eggs in a **stream.** Some of the eggs have new fish growing inside them.

Alevin

Fry

Smolt

This fish, called an **alevin,** has just **hatched** from its egg. The egg **yolk** is still joined to his stomach. It will provide food for the young fish.

Fully grown   Going home   Spawning

Fry

By springtime, the young fish is a **fry**. His stored food is almost gone, so he swims in the **fresh water** of the **stream** looking for insects and **plankton** to eat.

Alevin   Fry   Smolt

Millions of salmon fry live in the cold,
mountain stream. Many are eaten
by birds and other fish, but others
may live there for several years.

Fully grown Going home Spawning

Smolt

The young salmon are now as big as a human finger. They are called **smolt**. They leave the **stream** and start the long journey to the sea to find new food and grow into adults.

Alevin

Fry

Smolt

The trip is dangerous. The smolt
swim under logs and around boats.
Their bodies change to get ready for
the salty sea. Many die on the way.

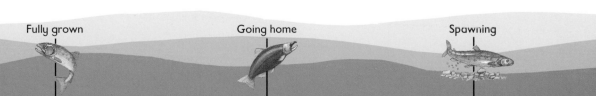

Fully grown   Going home   Spawning

Life in the Sea

The river gets wider. The water begins to smell salty as the salmon nears the sea. He pushes through the water with his strong tail.

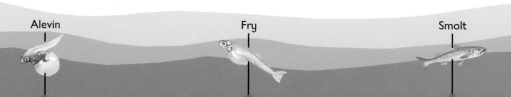

Alevin

Fry

Smolt

There are new dangers waiting for the salmon in the sea. This **tern** has just caught a small fish to eat.

Fully grown Going home Spawning

Danger from Animals

The salmon swims north to the cold sea near Alaska. He finds many new things to eat. He eats plenty of food and grows bigger and stronger.

Alevin

Fry

Smolt

Other sea animals, like this seal, try to catch and eat salmon. This salmon is lucky. None of the hungry animals catch him.

Fully grown

Going home

Spawning

Danger from People

The salmon is swimming far out into the deep ocean water. He feeds on shrimp, squid, small fish, and sea animals.

Alevin

Fry

Smolt

People can also be a danger to the salmon. This boat catches fish in its nets. The fish will be sold and eaten.

Fully grown

Going home

Spawning

Fully Grown

The salmon is now fully grown. He finds his way back to the river he left several years before. He begins the hard journey back **upstream**.

Alevin

Fry

Smolt

The salmon needs to be strong,
because the water keeps pushing
him back. He uses his tail to help
him leap over rocks and waterfalls.

Fully grown

Going home

Spawning

Going Home

Many other salmon are swimming up the river, too. They are now ready to **spawn.** As the salmon swim **upstream**, their skin becomes bright red. Their teeth grow sharp and pointed.

Alevin

Fry

Smolt

The salmon are in a hurry. They do
not eat on their way, but this hungry
bear is about to eat one of them!

Fully grown   Going home   Spawning

Salmon can find the right **stream** by remembering its smell. By autumn, hundreds of salmon have reached the streams where they were born.

Alevin

Fry

Smolt

The male fish have sharp, black
snouts. The females are fat with
eggs. They are ready to **spawn**.

Fully grown

Going home

Spawning

Spawning

The female uses her tail to dig a nest in the **gravel** on the bed of the **stream.** She lets thousands of eggs fall from her body into the nest.

Alevin

Fry

Smolt

The male swims after her and **fertilizes** the eggs. The female uses her tail to cover the nest with more gravel. They may make many nests.

Fully grown

Going home

Spawning

Journey's End

The salmon are tired and weak after their long, difficult swim up the river. It is easy for this bald eagle and other animals to catch them.

Alevin

Fry

Smolt

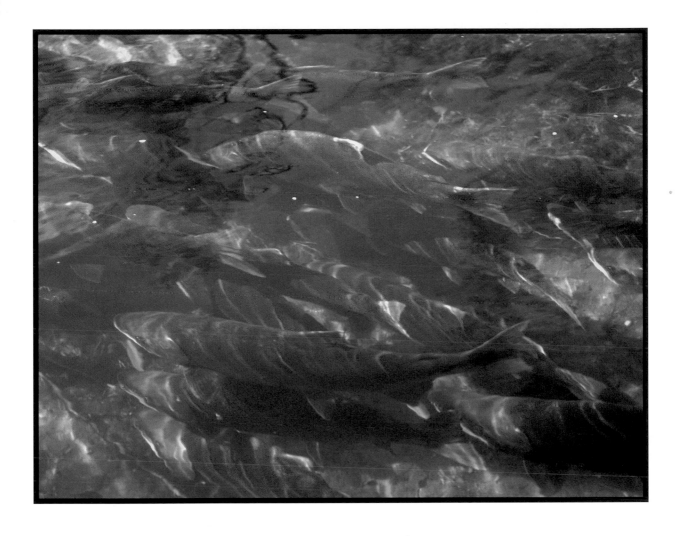

The salmon die soon after their eggs are laid. In ten weeks' time, the eggs will **hatch**. Thousands of new, tiny salmon will swim in the **stream.**

Fully grown   Going home   Spawning

Life Cycle

Alevin

1

Fry

2

Smolt

3

Fully grown

4

Spawning

5

Journey's end

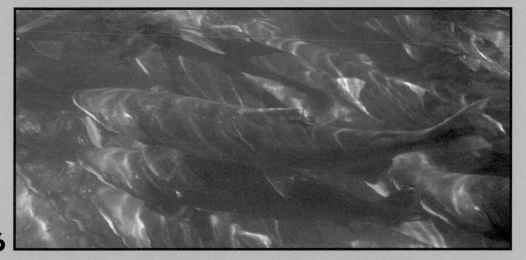

6

Fact File

A salmon's journey from the ocean back to the stream may be very long. Some salmon may travel as far as the distance from Chicago to California!

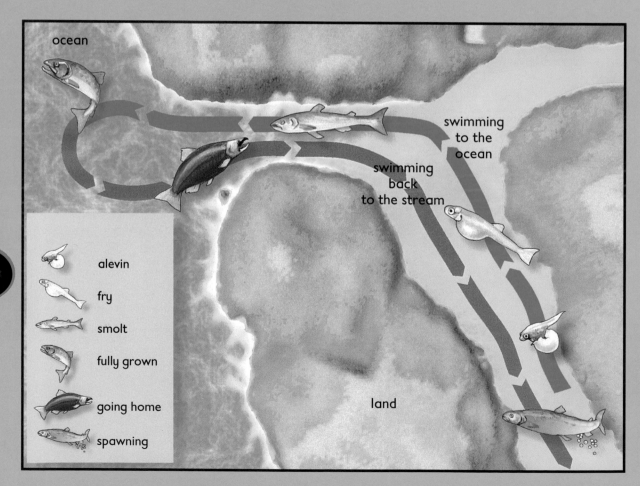

ocean

swimming
to the
ocean

swimming
back
to the stream

alevin

fry

smolt

fully grown

going home

spawning

land

Glossary

alevin salmon that has just come out of its egg
  (You say AL-uh-vin.)
fertilize when cells from a male fish join with eggs from
  a female to make baby fish
fresh water   water in streams, rivers, and lakes that
  does not taste salty
fry   young salmon
gravel small, rounded piece of rock
hatch   to break out of an egg
plankton   very tiny plants and animals that live
  in water
salt water   water that contains salt, such as ocean
  water
smolt young salmon that is ready to swim to the sea
snout   nose and mouth, when both stick out together
sockeye small, red salmon that is good to eat
spawn   when male and female salmon lay and fertilize
  eggs
stream   flowing water that is smaller than a river
tern   sea bird that looks like a seagull but is smaller
unique   different in a special way
upstream   against the flow of the water
yolk   store of food inside an egg

More Books to Read

Crewe, Sabrina. *The Salmon.* Austin, Tex.: Raintree Steck-Vaughn, 1996. An older reader can help you with this book.

Krulik, Nancy E. *The Magic School Bus Goes Upstream: A Book about Salmon Migration.* Madison, Wis.: Demco Media, Limited, 1997.

Savage, Stephen. *Salmon.* Austin, Tex.: Raintree Steck-Vaughn, 1995.

Index